Professor Brainstorm's

Sounds Like Fun

A **Science is Fun** book

Professor Brainstorm Books

Rick Turton

Illustrations by Sam Turton

Published by
Professor Brainstorm Books
5 Barmoor Bank, Morpeth, Northumberland, NE61 6LD
www.profbrainstorm.co.uk

Author: Rick Turton
Illustrations: Sam Turton

Photography: Focal Point Photography
www.focalpointphotography.co.uk
Page Layout: Sam Turton Designs
www.samturtondesigns.co.uk

Anyone undertaking any of the experiments described in this book does so entirely
at their own risk. Children should be supervised at all times by a responsible adult.
General warnings are given in the text, but whether or not a warning is given, it is
the responsibility of the reader always to take appropriate precautions and to exercise
due care. No responsibility for any consequences, however caused, will be accepted
by the author or Professor Brainstorm Books.

A CIP catalogue record for this book is available from the British Library.

ISBN: 978-0-9563367-0-5

Printed and bound in the UK
by MPG Biddles Ltd, Bodmin, Cornwall

Contents

Before You Start

Yes, I know you want to start the experiments right now, but there are a few important things to consider before doing any experiment. So please read the next two pages before you do anything else.

Be Safe

- Science experiments can be dangerous - so always tell an adult what you are doing before you begin the experiment.

- Read the instructions carefully before you start each experiment.

- Ask an adult for help if you need to use sharp scissors or electrical items - or if you are not quite sure what you have to do.

Be A Good Scientist

- When you are doing any science experiment it is important to look (and listen) carefully to see what is happening.

- If you measure something, do it twice - just to make sure you haven't made a mistake.

- When you notice something - or have measured something - write it down.

What Do I Need?

- Read the *What You Need* box for the experiment - and make sure you have all of the equipment before you start.

- You will probably already have most of the things that you need - either at home or in the classroom.

- If you don't have exactly the right equipment, don't worry. You may be able to use something similar instead.

Some of these experiments are rather noisy. This may make your Mum, Dad, brother or sister very angry. If they complain, tell them you are doing a science experiment. If they still complain, try one of the quieter experiments - until they are in a better mood.

How Does It Work?

- Science experiments are even more fun when you find out how they work.

- Each experiment in this book has a box explaining how the experiment works. If there are some words which you don't understand, look in the *Glossary* at the back of the book. (The meanings of the words in **bold** type are explained in the *Glossary*.)

- Once you understand how the experiment works, you may even be able to invent some similar experiments of your own.

What If It Doesn't Work?

- I have tried all of these experiments personally in my Brainstorm Laboratory - so I know that they do all work. However, sometimes you may find that your experiment just doesn't seem to work.

- If your experiment doesn't work, read through the instructions again very carefully. Is there something that you haven't done quite right? (It may also be helpful to read the *How Does It Work* section as this may help you to see where you are going wrong.)

- If it still doesn't work, don't get too frustrated. Try another experiment instead. You may find that the experiment works if you try it again a few days later. (And when you do get it to work, you may discover why it didn't work the first time.)

Science is Fun

Some of these experiments will amaze you.
Others will make you think.
But all of them should be FUN.
So I hope you have lots of fun doing these experiments.

Professor Brainstorm

Crisp Tube Bonkos

Bonkos are a simple type of **percussion** instrument. (This means that you make a sound by hitting them.) In this experiment we are going to make several bonkos - and we will investigate how the sound changes if the bonkos are long or short.

How to make your Crisp Tube Bonkos

1 Collect together 4 or 5 crisp tubes. If possible, try to find ones of different lengths.

2 If two of the tubes are the same length, ask an adult to cut off the top of one of the tubes to make it a bit shorter than the other one. Put sticky tape around the rim so that there are no rough edges.

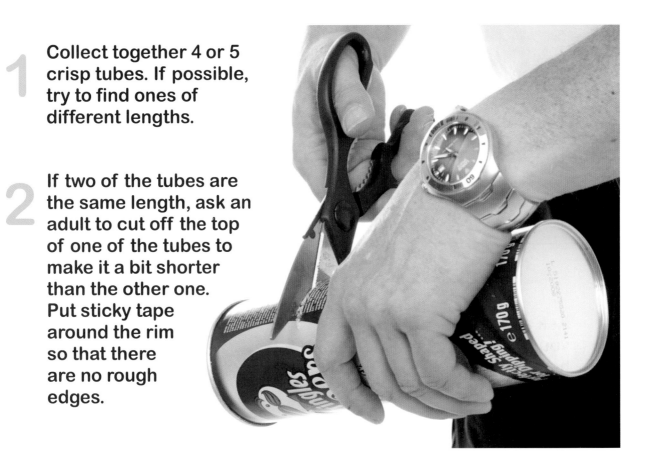

3 Cut down the tubes so that they are all different sizes. (You can leave one tube the original size.)

4 Decorate the tubes using wrapping paper. (Or you could use plain paper and draw your own designs.)

5 Now your bonkos are ready to play. Hold one of the tubes upside down and hit the metal base of the tube with a spoon. Do the same thing with each of the other tubes. Do they make different sounds?

6 Ask a few of your friends to help you play your bonkos. Now you have a bonko orchestra!

How does it work?

- When you hit the base of the crisp tube, the base of the tube **vibrates**. This makes the air inside the tube vibrate as well.

- If the tube is short, the air vibrates more quickly. This makes a sound with a **higher** pitch.

- If the tube is long, the air vibrates slowly. This produces a sound with a **low pitch**.

- So if we use a long tube the pitch is low. If it is a shorter tube the pitch is higher.

Now try this

- Ask an adult to cut the metal base off one of the crisp tubes - so now you have a tube which is open at both ends.

- Use some sticky tape to join this tube to the open end of another crisp tube - to make a really long bonko. What sort of sound do you think this bonko will make?

- If you have enough crisp tubes you can add even more open tubes to make an even longer bonko. Really long bonkos make an incredibly low-pitched sound.

Fun Facts: Bamboo Bonkos

- Bonkos are used for making traditional music in many different cultures all around the world - including Africa, Asia and South America.

- Traditional bonkos are usually made out of bamboo - not crisp tubes!

- Bamboo bonkos are sometimes played by hitting them with sticks, but often they are stamped against the ground - so they are sometimes called *stamping tubes*.

Try this as well

All you need for this experiment is a 30cm plastic ruler. (It works best if you can find a really bendy ruler.)

- Place the ruler on a table top so that about 10cm of the ruler is sticking over the edge.

- Use one hand to press the ruler down against the edge of the table. (Your hand should be very close to the edge of the table.) With your other hand, press the end of the ruler down about 2cm, then let it go.

- The end of the ruler vibrates for a few seconds - and it makes a sound.

- Now move the ruler slightly so that there is just 9cm hanging over the edge. Make the ruler vibrate again. Did you notice that the pitch is higher?

- Move the ruler so that there is 8cm sticking out, then 7cm, and so on. As you make the length of the vibrating part shorter, the pitch gets higher.

- We can see that the end of the ruler is vibrating. It is vibrating extremely quickly.

- Move the ruler so that about 15cm is hanging over the edge. It may be difficult to hear it this time, because the pitch is so low. You should also notice that the ruler is vibrating more slowly than before.

- So as the vibrating part of the ruler gets longer, the vibrations become slower, and the pitch gets lower.

What have we found out?

- **Long objects vibrate slowly and make a sound with a low pitch.**

- **Short objects vibrate quickly and make a sound with a high pitch.**

Laughing Chicken

In this experiment we are going to make a sound in a rather unusual way. You will be amazed at the strange sounds you can make with just a yogurt pot and a piece of string. The Laughing Chicken is very easy to make - and it really does make a sound like a chicken!

How to make your Laughing Chicken

1   Ask an adult to use the sharp point of the scissors to make a small hole in the bottom of the yogurt pot.

2   Cut a short length of string (about 15-20 cm is fine). **Thread one end of the string through the hole in the bottom of the yogurt pot and tie a knot in the end of the string (so the knot is on the inside of the yogurt pot).** If you have difficulty getting the string through the hole, try wrapping a piece of sticky tape round the end of the string.

3 Cut out a piece of paper which is just a bit smaller than one side of the yogurt pot. Draw a chicken on the paper, then stick it on the front of your yogurt pot.

4 Make the string nice and wet. (You can dip the string in a jug of water - but be careful not to get water on your picture.)

5 Now you are ready to make your chicken laugh. Hold the rim of the yogurt pot in one hand and pull the string between the thumb and forefinger of your other hand. (Don't pull too hard! The idea is that your hand should slide down the string.) Does it make a sound like a chicken?

Now try this

- What happens if you rub a piece of wet string? Try it. Can you hear anything? If not, put it really close to your ear. You should hear a tiny squeaky sound.

- When you make a *Laughing Chicken*, the yogurt pot makes lots of air vibrate. This produces a **loud** sound. Without the yogurt pot the sound is very **quiet**.

- Using your *Laughing Chicken* try holding the string gently between your finger and thumb. Now grip the string more tightly. Did you notice any difference in the sound?

- When you grip the string tightly it makes a sound with a **higher pitch** than if you hold the string more loosely.
  (We will do more experiments to investigate how **tension** affects the pitch in the *Elastic Band Guitar* experiment.)

- Does the sound change if you use a larger container? Or a smaller one? Usually a large container makes a sound with a **lower pitch** than a small one. The photograph on the cover shows me using a very large *Laughing Chicken*. (However, this one sounds more like a laughing giant!)

Fun Facts: Silent Fireworks

- When we hear a sound, our ear is actually detecting vibrations in the air. If it is a really loud sound - like a firework exploding - you may be able to feel the vibrations.

- Since there is no air on the Moon, if you went to the Moon and set off some fireworks, you would see lots of flashes - but you wouldn't hear any BANGS!

How does it work?

- As you pull down on the string, your finger and thumb tend to stick and slip (rather than sliding smoothly) down the string.

- This means that the bottom of the yogurt pot gets pulled down a little, then springs back up, then gets pulled down again, and so on.

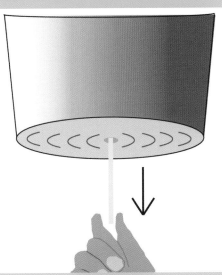

- So the bottom of the yogurt pot **vibrates**. (All of this happens very quickly - and the movements of the yogurt pot are very small - so you can't actually see it vibrating!)

- As the bottom of the yogurt pot vibrates, it makes all of the air inside the yogurt pot vibrate as well.

- These vibrations travel through the air to our ears.

- A larger container makes more air vibrate - so the sound is **louder**.

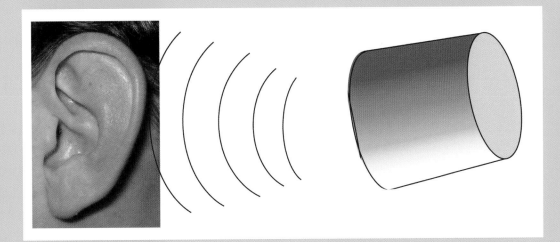

What have we found out?

- **Sounds are produced when something vibrates.**

- **We hear a sound because the vibrations travel through the air.**

Elastic Band Guitar

It is often difficult to see what is vibrating when we make a sound - but on a guitar we can actually see the strings vibrate. In this experiment we are going to make a simple guitar, and explore how the sound changes when we alter the thickness and tension of the elastic band.

How to make an Elastic Band Guitar

1 Stretch an elastic band between your thumb and fingers. Pluck the elastic band using your other hand. You should hear a 'twang' sound - and you can see the elastic band vibrating.

2 Remove the lid from the margarine tub and stretch an elastic band across the open container. Pluck the elastic band again. What is different about the sound that it makes this time?

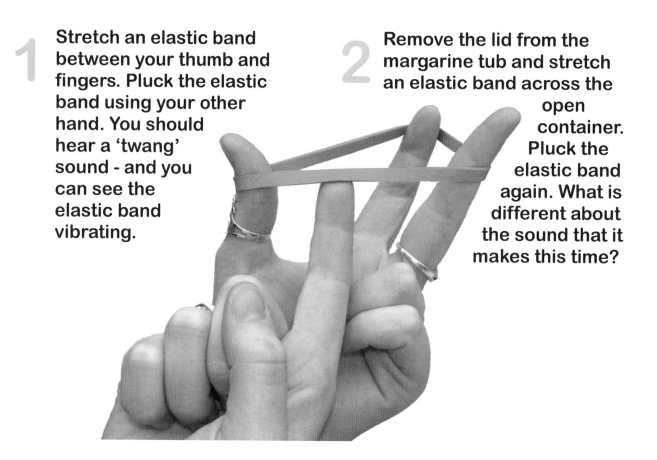

3 Slide your finger between the elastic band and the side of the margarine tub. Pull your finger outwards slightly so that the elastic band becomes more stretched. Does the sound change as you stretch the elastic band?

4 Repeat the experiment, but this time use a thicker elastic band. Or a thinner one. (If possible try to find elastic bands which are about the same length when they are not stretched.) Does the thickness of the elastic band alter the sound?

15

How does it work?

- When you pluck a stretched elastic band, the elastic band **vibrates** and produces a sound.

- By stretching the elastic band across a margarine tub, the air in the container vibrates as well - and the sound gets **louder**.

- On a real guitar, the main body of the instrument is just an empty wooden box. When you pluck a string, the air inside the guitar vibrates, so the sound is louder. (An electric guitar does not have any air inside it - because in this case electricity is used to **amplify** the sound.)

- When the elastic band is only slightly stretched it makes slow, lazy vibrations - producing a sound with a **low pitch**.

- When the elastic band is stretched further, the vibrations are faster - so the pitch of the sound is **higher**.

- On a real guitar we can change the pitch by turning the **tuning** keys.

- The thickness of the elastic band also affects the pitch. A thick elastic band produces a lower pitch than a thin one.

- If you look at the strings on a guitar, you will see that the strings which make the lowest notes are thicker than the ones which play the high notes.

Now try this

- Instead of using a margarine tub, try using a different container - such as a cardboard box or a mug. You may notice that the sound changes in another way. This is called the sound quality or **timbre**.

- The same thing happens with real musical instruments. Guitars and banjos are both **stringed instruments** - but if you play the same note on each instrument it sounds quite different. This is because the instruments are different in shape and size - so they produce sounds with a different timbre.

What have we found out?

- Sounds become louder if we make more air vibrate.

- Increasing the tension of a guitar string (or an elastic band) makes the pitch higher.

- Increasing the thickness of a guitar string (or an elastic band) makes the pitch lower.

Straw Oboe

What you need
Drinking straw
Scissors

Did you know that you can make a musical instrument using just a drinking straw? Well, it makes a great sound, but not everyone thinks it sounds like music. So don't be surprised if after a few minutes someone tells you to **shut up!**

How to make your Straw Oboe

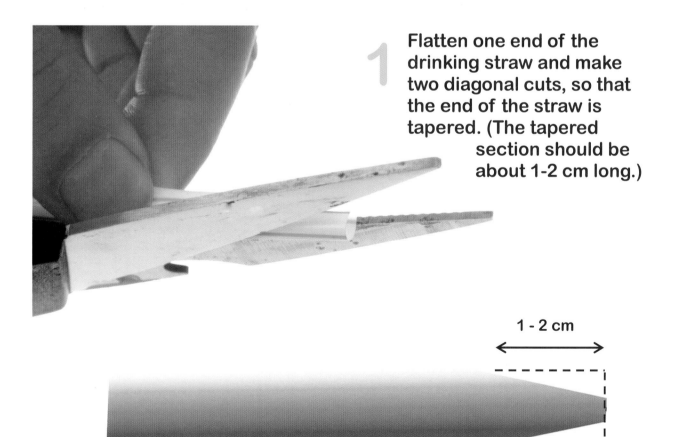

1 Flatten one end of the drinking straw and make two diagonal cuts, so that the end of the straw is tapered. (The tapered section should be about 1-2 cm long.)

1 - 2 cm

2 Put the tapered section of the straw in your mouth and blow gently. It may take several tries before you manage to make a sound. (I find it works best if you put most of the tapered part inside your mouth and squeeze down gently on the straw with your lips. You don't need to bite the straw!)

3 Once you have mastered the art of playing your straw oboe, try making some more using straws of different lengths. Does the length of the straw affect the sound that the straw oboe makes?

4 Now that you have several straw oboes of different lengths, ask your friends to help you play them. You might even be able to play a tune.

How does it work?

- As you blow, the two tapered ends of the straw **vibrate** - they open and close very quickly. You will probably be able to feel this vibration on your lips. (In fact, after a minute or so of playing, the vibrations will make your lips feel quite tingly.)

- If you make the drinking straw longer or shorter, the **pitch** changes. As you may have already discovered in the *Crisp Tube Bonko* experiment, a long column of air vibrates slowly, so it makes a sound with a **low pitch**. A shorter column of air vibrates more quickly, so the pitch is **higher**.

- A real oboe works in a similar way - but instead of using the two tapered ends of a straw, it uses a *double reed*. (Although it is called a *reed*, it is actually made from bamboo!)

- When a musician blows between the reeds, the reed vibrates, just like the ends of the drinking straw.

Fun Facts: Large and Small

An orchestra is made up of many different musical instruments. Some of the instruments are similar to one another, but vary in size. For example, a piccolo is like a tiny flute. Since it is smaller than a flute, it can play much higher notes. Can you find other instruments which look similar to one another, but which make sounds with a different pitch?

Now try this

Now that you have made a sort of 'oboe', why not try making a trombone as well? To make the trombone all you need is:

- a small (about 500ml) plastic drink bottle, and
- a piece of copper pipe or plastic tubing. The pipe needs to be narrow enough so that it fits inside the neck of the bottle, and long enough so that about 10cm sticks out of the top of the bottle.

- Fill the bottle with water, leaving a space of about 2cm at the top.

- Insert the pipe into the bottle and blow gently across the top of the pipe. (It is important to blow *across* rather than *into* the pipe.) You should be able to hear a faint sound.

- Keep the end of the pipe close to your lips and slowly lower the bottle. Can you hear the pitch change?

- As you move the bottle downwards, the length of the air column becomes longer - and so the pitch gets lower.

You can make the sound much louder if you use a hairdryer to blow across the top of the pipe. However, using a hairdryer when there is water around can potentially be very dangerous. DO NOT TRY THIS UNLESS YOU HAVE ADULT SUPERVISION.

What have we found out?

- Sounds are made when something vibrates.
- Long tubes make a sound with a low pitch, short tubes make a sound with a high pitch.

Have you ever wished that you had super powers? Wouldn't it be great if you could hear really quiet sounds that no one else could hear? In this experiment we will find out how to hear very quiet sounds even when the sound source is quite far away.

How you can get
Super Hearing

1 Firstly, we are going to find out how good your hearing is without *Super Hearing*. Play some music on your MP3 player. Put one earphone in your ear and turn the volume down until you can only just hear it.

2 Take the earphone out of your ear. Move it slowly away from your ear until you can no longer hear the music.

3 Ask a friend to measure the distance of the earphone from your ear when you can just about hear the sound. (If you can still hear the music when the earphone is more than 10cm from your ear, you will have to turn the volume down a bit more and start again.)

4 Find a cardboard tube which is about 20-30cm long. (The tube from a roll of cling film or aluminium foil is ideal.) Hold one end of the tube close to your ear and put the earphone at the other end of the tube. Even though the earphone is much further from your ear than it was before, you should still be able to hear the music quite clearly.

5 Repeat the experiment using an even longer tube. (You could use a poster tube or a piece of plastic pipe.) Can you still hear the music?

How does it work?

● When you hear a sound, your ear is actually detecting **vibrations** in the air. If the sound is very **quiet**, these vibrations are usually very small.

● Sound from the earphones normally spreads out in all directions. So as you move the earphones further from your ear, the vibrations become smaller and smaller - until they are too small for your ear to detect.

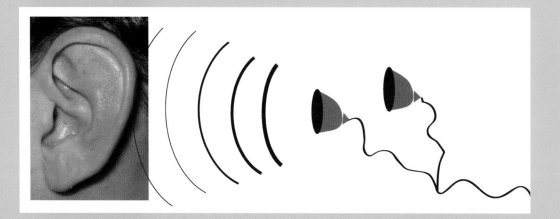

● When you put the earphone at the end of the cardboard tube, the vibrations travel through the air in the tube - but they can't spread out in other directions.

● The vibrations which reach your ear are nearly as big as they were when they left the earphone. So you can still hear the sound, even if the tube is quite long.

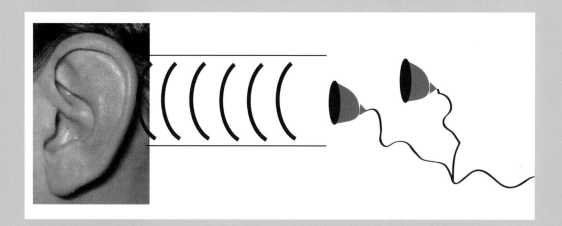

● How long can you make the tube? I have tried this experiment using a piece of drainpipe which was over 4 metres long - and I could clearly hear someone whispering at the other end.

Now try this

You can use the same idea to make your own **stethoscope**. (This is an instrument which a doctor uses to listen to sounds inside your body.)

- To make your stethoscope you need a plastic funnel and a piece of garden hosepipe about 50cm long. (Make sure you ask your parents before cutting a piece off their hosepipe! Also make sure that it is the type of hosepipe which looks like a rigid cylinder. The type which squashes flat does not work very well.)

- Push the narrow end of the funnel into one end of the hosepipe. Hold the other end of the hosepipe close to your ear.

- Now hold the wide end of the funnel against your chest. Can you hear your heart beating?

- If you move the funnel a bit further down your body you may also be able to hear your tummy rumble!

What have we found out?

- If you move away from a sound source, the sound usually becomes quieter (until it is so quiet you can no longer hear it.)

- If the sound travels through a tube, you can hear very quiet sounds from quite far away.

Where's That Sound?

What you need
Blindfold
Metal spoons

Why are two ears better than one? Our ears not only hear sounds, they can also tell us where a sound is coming from. Are you good at identifying the direction of a sound? You can make this experiment into a game to play with a friend.

How to play
Where's That Sound?

1 Ask your friend to sit on a chair in the middle of the room. Put a blindfold over his or her eyes. (Make sure that the blindfold does not cover their ears!) Tell them that they have to *keep their head still*.

2 Stand to one side of them, about 30cm from their ear. Tap the spoons together gently and ask them to point in the direction from which the sound is coming. Did they guess correctly?

3 Move quietly until you are directly behind them. Tap the spoons together again. Did they guess the right direction this time? (Remind them that they cannot turn their head.)

4 Try tapping the spoons together in different positions - in front of them, directly above their head, or even underneath the chair. Each time make a note of whether they get the direction right or not.

5 Try the experiment again, but this time tell them that they can move their head. Do they manage to do better this time?

6 Now swap places. Put on the blindfold and ask your friend to tap the spoons together. (And remember to keep your head still.)

How does it work?

- Since we have an ear on each side of our head, most people are quite good at recognizing whether a sound is coming from their right or left side.

- If someone makes a sound near your right ear, the **volume** of the sound reaching your right ear is slightly **louder** than that reaching your left ear. (Also the sound has to travel slightly further to reach your left ear, so your right ear hears the sound slightly earlier than your left ear.)

- We are not usually aware of hearing different things in different ears - our brain just works it all out for us automatically.

- It is much harder to tell whether a sound is coming from behind, above or in front of us - because in these cases we hear just about the same sound in each ear.

- However, if you turn your head, you should be able to work out where the sound is coming from.

Fun Facts: Hearing Danger

Having two ears is very useful as it can help us to avoid dangerous situations. Cavemen would have found this useful, because if they heard a sabre-tooth tiger roar, they needed to know which direction it was coming from - so that they could run in the opposite direction!

Although you probably won't ever have to run away from a tiger, you can use your ears in other dangerous situations - such as listening for traffic when you are waiting to cross a road.

Now try this

- Cut two lengths of hosepipe, each about 50cm long, and fit a plastic funnel into one end of each hose. (Each one is like the *Homemade Stethoscope* that you made in the *Super Hearing* experiment.)

- Use some sticky tape to hold the two hosepipes together - making sure that the ends with the funnels are pointing in opposite directions.

- Place the other ends of the tubes close to each ear.

- Play *Where's That Sound?* again. Make sure you tap the spoons together close to the open end of the funnel.

- If your friend makes a sound near the funnel on your left side, you will hear the sound in your right ear. If they make a sound on your right side you will think it is coming from your left.

What have we found out?

- We can use our ears to tell us which direction a sound is coming from.

Ringing In Your Ears

In this experiment we are going to make a sound like a ringing bell. The amazing thing is that only you can hear it! This experiment is really simple, but it is so cool you will want to show it to all your friends.

How to make your Ears Ring

1 Cut a piece of string about 60cm long. Tie one end of the string tightly around the handle of the spoon.

2 Hold the end of the string up in the air so that the spoon dangles from the other end. Allow the spoon to gently hit a hard surface, such as the edge of a table. You should hear a quiet ringing sound.

3 Now hold the end of the string against your ear - and again allow the spoon to gently hit the edge of the table.

4 Wow! Did you hear that? It sounds like someone is ringing a bell INSIDE your head. (The first time I did this experiment I had to do it again and again just to convince myself that it was really happening.)

5 Now ask a friend to try the experiment with you. If you hold the string against your ear, all they will hear is a quiet ringing sound. They won't believe how loud the sound is until they try it for themselves. Isn't it amazing that two people standing next to each other can hear the same sound so differently?

31

How does it work?

- Most materials - including air and string - are made of tiny particles called **molecules**.

- When you hit the spoon against a hard object, the spoon starts to **vibrate** - which makes the air molecules near the spoon bump into one another.

- As these molecules bump into other molecules, the sound spreads out - and after a fraction of a second some of these molecules bump into your **eardrum** - producing tiny vibrations - which you hear as a **quiet** sound.

- The vibrations from the spoon also travel along the piece of string. When you press the string against your ear, your ear feels the vibrations in the string.

- Since the molecules in the string are much closer together than the molecules in air, the vibrations that have travelled through the string are much bigger than those that have travelled through the air - so the sound is much louder.

Fun Facts:
Using Sound to Get Rid of Moles

If your Dad gets mad because some moles have been digging holes in his lawn, you can impress him by using science to chase the moles away.

- Push a metal pipe down one of the mole holes. You need to leave about 30cm of the pipe sticking up above the ground.

- Get an old baked bean can and turn it upside down so that it fits over the top of the pipe.

- When the wind blows, the can clangs and bangs against the metal pipe, making a ringing sound which travels right down the mole hole.

- The moles soon get fed up with the horrible noise - so they go somewhere else - and dig up someone else's garden.

Now try this

- Repeat the experiment - but instead of using string, try it with some thin cotton or a shoelace.

- You can even try it with a strip of plastic cut from a carrier bag. (This works best if you hold the strip of plastic directly over your ear hole.)

- Do any of these materials work better than the string?

Try this as well

Another way to investigate how sounds travel along a string is to make a string telephone. You may be surprised how well this one works.

- Cut a piece of string about 2m long. Thread a large yogurt pot onto one end of the string and tie a knot inside the yogurt pot. Do the same thing at the other end of the string.

- Ask a friend to hold one of the yogurt pots really close to their ear.

- Now pull the string taut, and whisper very quietly into the other yogurt pot. Can your friend hear what you are saying?

- Just like the *Ringing In Your Ears* experiment, the vibrations travel along the string. But you have to keep the string really taut to make it work.

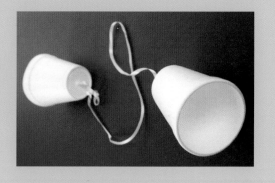

What have we found out?

- Sound usually travels better through solid materials than it does through air.

Be Quiet!

What you need
CD player
Headphones
Bubble wrap
Tea towel
Kitchen roll

Do you ever get fed up with all the noise? Noisy brothers and sisters, noisy traffic. Wouldn't it be great if you could just have some peace and quiet? In this experiment we are going to find out how to make things quieter.

How to play Be Quiet!

1 Put on your headphones and turn on some music.

2 Slide a sheet of bubble wrap between your ear and the headphones. Listen again. Does the music sound any quieter? (It is sometimes easier to hear the difference as you pull the bubble wrap out.)

3 Fold each sheet of bubble wrap in half - so now you have double the thickness of bubble wrap on each ear. Listen again. Does the music sound even quieter?

4 Try again using even more layers of bubble wrap. (Make sure that each time you listen to the music you use the same thickness of bubble wrap on each ear.)

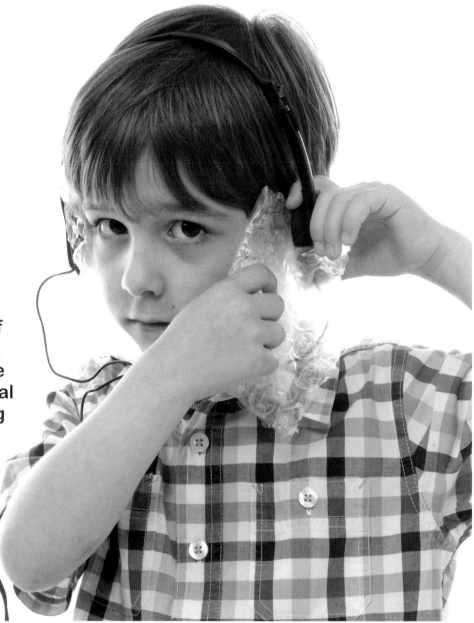

5 Repeat the experiment using other materials, such as a tea towel, or sheets of kitchen roll. Which is the best material for stopping the sound?

6 Can you think of any reasons why some materials are better at stopping sound than others?
(For example, one sheet of bubble wrap is much thicker than one sheet of kitchen roll. Would it be a fairer test to compare the same thickness of kitchen roll and bubble wrap?)

35

How does it work?

- If you have done some of the other experiments in this book you will know that sound is really a **vibration**.

- It is difficult for these vibrations to travel through certain types of material. These materials are good at absorbing - or **muffling** - sound.

- If we use several layers of these materials, they absorb even more of the sound - so the **volume** of the sound reaching our ears is very **quiet**.

- There is another reason why the sound becomes quieter as we use more layers of material. Can you guess what it is?
(Hint: you may know the answer if you have done the *Super Hearing* experiment.)

People who work in noisy environments have to wear special headphones - or 'ear defenders' - to avoid damaging their hearing.

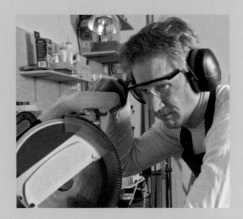

Answer: As you use more layers of material, the headphones get pushed further from your ears. So the sound is quieter because it has to travel further to reach your ears.

Fun Facts: Sound Guns

You may think that 'sound guns' are something that you would only find in a science fiction comic - but several police forces have experimented with the idea of using loud, high-pitched sound to disperse crowds of rioters or football hooligans. If you are hit by one of these 'sound bullets' you get an intense pain in your ears - and you may even feel sick and dizzy.

Now try this

- Put a small music player into a shoe box. (The music player could be a radio, an MP3 player with speakers, or perhaps a mobile phone.)

- Close the lid of the shoe box and check that you can hear the music quite clearly. (If not, you will need to turn the volume up slightly.)

- Put several layers of bubble wrap in the box. Place your music player on the bubble wrap in the middle of the box, then add more layers of bubble wrap on top. Close the lid. Can you still hear the music? Is it as loud as before?

- Try filling the box with different materials. You could use a small towel, some scrunched up kitchen roll, or polystyrene packaging. Which material is best at stopping the sound?

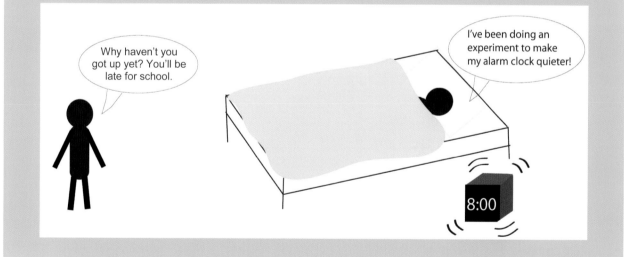

What have we found out?

- **Some materials are good at muffling sound.**

- **Using a thicker layer (or more layers) of material blocks out more of the sound.**

Dancing Krispies

Whenever anything makes a sound, it is actually vibrating. Usually these vibrations are far too small to see, but in this experiment we are going to use the vibrations to make your breakfast cereal dance.

How to make your Krispies Dance

1 Cut the freezer bag open - to make one large sheet of plastic - and place it over the top of the bowl. The sheet must be large enough to completely cover the top of the bowl. If there are any gaps you will need to find a larger bag - or a smaller bowl.
(You can use cling film instead of a freezer bag, but I find that this experiment works better with a slightly thicker sheet of plastic.)

2 Use some sticky tape to fasten the freezer bag to the sides of the bowl, making sure that the plastic film is stretched really taut.

3 Sprinkle a handful of puffed rice cereal over the stretched plastic film.

4 Put the speaker of the CD player next to the bowl. Play some dance music or rock music - you need something with a good powerful beat - and turn up the volume really LOUD. Your krispies should start to jiggle about.

39

How does it work?

- Loud music from the CD player makes the air inside the bowl **vibrate** - which makes the plastic film vibrate.

- Although these vibrations are far too small for us to see directly, they are large enough to make the breakfast cereal shake about.

For another way to 'see' the vibrations, try the *Make An Ear* experiment.

Now try this

Try repeating this experiment using different types of food.
I have tried it with:

- other types of breakfast cereal,
- sugar,
- oats,
- salt,
- uncooked pasta.

- Which types of food are the best dancers?

- Why do you think some types of food shake about more than others?

Items which are light usually shake about more than ones which are heavy. However, things like grains of salt - which are very light - are also very small, so they are difficult to see. I think krispies make the best dancers because they are both lightweight and large enough to see, but you might be able to find something which is even better.

Fun Facts: Good Vibrations

- Dame Evelyn Glennie is a world-famous musician - despite the fact that she has been profoundly deaf since she was 12 years old.

- She has taught herself to 'hear' music by feeling the vibrations that it produces. She often plays barefoot, so that she can feel the vibrations through her feet.

- Most of us are not as good at feeling vibrations as Dame Evelyn Glennie - but one sound that you will be able to feel is a really low note played on a church organ. (You won't even need to take your shoes off to feel it!)

WHIFF

PONG

When I said listen carefully, I meant listen with your ears - not with your feet!

What have we found out?

- Sounds are made when something vibrates.

- Really loud sounds can make other objects vibrate as well - such as pieces of breakfast cereal.

Balloon Bassoon

Making a balloon bassoon is quite difficult - you will probably need an adult to help you with several of the stages - but it makes such a great sound that it is well worth the effort. Make sure you read through all of the instructions carefully before you start.

How to make a Balloon Bassoon

1 Ask an adult to cut a length of PVC pipe about 30cm long. Use sandpaper to rub down any rough edges on the pipe.

2 Cut out a hole in the base of the yogurt pot. The hole should be just large enough for the PVC pipe to fit through. (Again you will need to ask an adult to help with this.)

42

3 Make a very small hole near the top rim of the yogurt pot. This hole needs to be just big enough for the straw to fit through.

4 Cut off the neck of the balloon. Stretch the remaining part of the balloon over the top of the yogurt pot, making sure that there are no gaps. The balloon forms something called a **diaphragm** (pronounced 'di-a-fram').

5 Insert the PVC pipe through the hole in the base of the yogurt pot and push it up gently so that the rubber diaphragm becomes slightly stretched. Keep the pipe in this position and use sticky tape to seal all the gaps between the yogurt pot and the PVC pipe.

Balloon Bassoon

6 Cut a length of straw about 6cm long and push it into the hole that you made near the top of the yogurt pot. (You will need to slide it in at an angle to get it past the PVC pipe.) Again use sticky tape to seal all the gaps.

7 Your balloon bassoon is now complete. Put your lips around the straw and blow. It should produce a really low-pitched sound - like a foghorn.

What to do if your Balloon Bassoon doesn't work

- Check to make sure that all the gaps have been sealed. The only place where you should feel any air coming out is the bottom of the PVC pipe.

- Make sure that the PVC pipe is really stretching the rubber diaphragm. Try pushing the PVC pipe upwards slightly as you blow. This will help to stretch the rubber diaphragm a bit more.

How does it work?

- When you blow into the straw, the only way the air can get out of the yogurt pot is by lifting up the balloon **diaphragm**.

- Each time a little bit of air squeezes between the diaphragm and the top of the PVC pipe, it causes the diaphragm to lift up.

- When you blow hard into the straw, a lot of air has to escape - so it lifts the diaphragm up and down very quickly. The diaphragm **vibrates**.

- Press your finger gently against the top of the PVC pipe (where it pushes against the diaphragm). Now blow through the straw. Can you feel the diaphragm vibrating?

Now try this

- Although the PVC pipe is fastened to the yogurt pot, you may be able to move the PVC pipe in and out by just a few millimetres.

- Try blowing into the straw as you gently push the PVC pipe upwards. (Don't push too hard or you may break the seal between the rubber and the yogurt pot.) Does the pitch change?

- Try it again, but this time pull the pipe downwards slightly as you blow. What happens to the pitch this time?

- As you push the pipe upwards, the **tension** in the **diaphragm** increases and the **pitch** becomes **higher**. If you pull the pipe downwards, the tension is reduced, and the pitch gets **lower**.

What have we found out?

- **When objects vibrate they make a sound.**

- **Increasing the tension in the diaphragm makes the pitch higher.**

- **Reducing the tension in the diaphragm makes the pitch lower.**

Make An Ear

What you need
CD player
Paper cup
Cling film
Torch
Plain paper
Cereal box
Sharp scissors
Sticky tape

In this experiment we are going to make an artificial ear. This ear won't actually be able to hear anything - but it will help to show us how a real ear works.

How to make an Artificial Ear

1 Cut out the bottom of a paper cup and stretch a piece of cling film over the end. Use sticky tape to ensure that the cling film is stretched really taut.

2 Place the paper cup about 2cm in front of the speaker of a CD player. (The end covered in cling film should be further away from the speaker.)

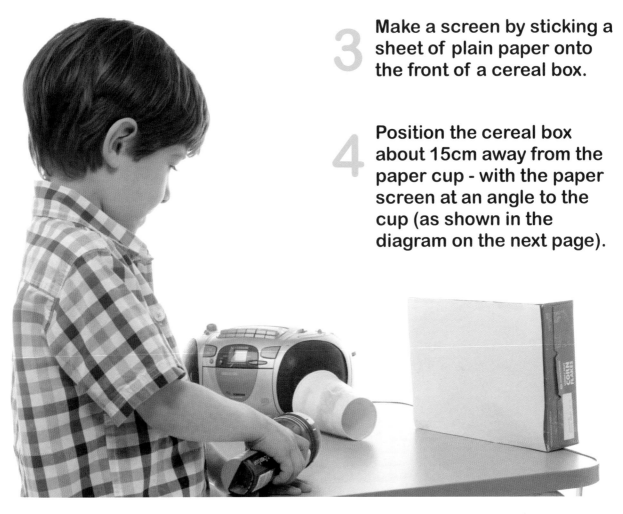

3 Make a screen by sticking a sheet of plain paper onto the front of a cereal box.

4 Position the cereal box about 15cm away from the paper cup - with the paper screen at an angle to the cup (as shown in the diagram on the next page).

5 Place the torch at a similar distance from the cup - but on the opposite side from the screen. Aim the torch so that the light reflects off the cling film and onto the paper screen. You should see a pattern similar to this ➡

(If you don't get anything like this, you need to adjust the positions of the torch and the cereal box until you do. It also helps if you can make the room fairly dark.)

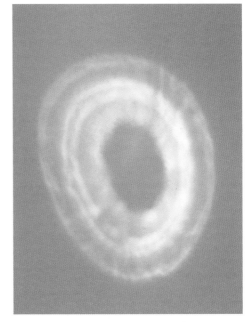

6 Play some music on the CD player. The pattern on the card should start to move about. (This works best if you use some music with a strong beat. If you can't see the patterns moving, turn the volume up a little.)

How does it work?

- Light from the torch is reflected off the cling film and shines on to the plain paper screen - producing a pattern on the screen.

- If you stretch or press on the cling film gently with your finger, you can see that the pattern on the screen changes.

- When you turn the CD player on, the music makes the cling film **vibrate**. Although the vibrations are too small for us to see directly, we can see that the cling film is moving because the reflected patterns are now constantly changing.

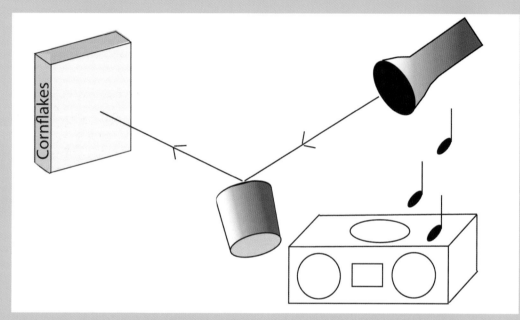

- Instead of cling film, your ear has a thin membrane of skin - called an **ear drum** - stretched across the passageway inside your ear.

- When a sound enters your ear, it makes your ear drum vibrate.

- Three tiny bones connect the ear drum to the cochlea. These bones **amplify** the vibrations.

- The cochlea converts the vibrations into tiny electrical signals - which travel along the auditory nerve to your brain.

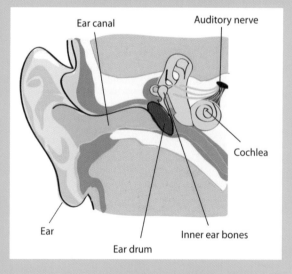

48

Fun Facts: What Can You Hear?

- Did you know that you can hear things that your Mum and Dad can't hear?

- As you get older it gets more difficult to hear really high-pitched sounds. In fact, by the time you are 25 you will not be able to hear some of the sounds that you can hear now.

Fun Facts: What Do Animals Hear?

- Animals like bats, mice and dogs can hear sounds with a much higher pitch than even children can hear?

- In contrast, elephants can hear sounds with a much lower pitch than we can hear.

- Elephants use very low-pitched sounds to communicate with other elephants - which may be as far as several kilometres away.

What have we found out?

- Sounds are really vibrations which travel through the air.

- We hear a sound when vibrations in the air make our ear drum vibrate.

Bouncing Sounds

What you need
MP3 player
Earphones
Chopping board
Tea towel
2 long cardboard
tubes

I f you shout in a large, empty room, your voice can bounce off the walls and come back to you. We call this an **echo**. In this experiment we are going to investigate how we can make sounds change direction by bouncing them off various objects.

How to
Bounce a Sound

1 Play some music on your MP3 player. Turn the volume right down so you can only just hear it when you put the earphone in your ear.

2 Place the earphone into the end of one of the cardboard tubes and hold the other end of the tube against your ear. Check that you can still hear the sound. Now lie this tube down on the table.

3 Hold the second tube close to your ear and position the other end of this tube close to the one on the table. The two tubes should be at an angle to one another, as shown in the photograph on the previous page. Can you hear the music? (It doesn't matter if you can't hear it.)

4 Keeping both tubes in the same position, ask a friend to hold a chopping board across the ends of the two tubes. Can you hear the music now?

5 Cover the chopping board with a tea towel. Listen again. Can you still hear the music? Is it as loud as before?

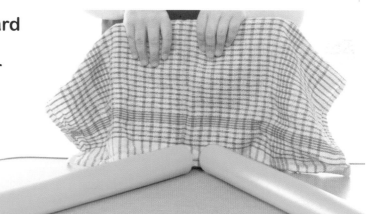

51

How does it work?

- If you have done the *Super Hearing* experiment you will already know that you can hear a **quiet** sound more easily when the sound travels through a tube.

- In this experiment we have used the chopping board to 'bounce' the sound from the first tube into the second one. (A better description is to say that the sound has been **reflected** off the chopping board.)

- When a sound that we make bounces back to us, we call it an **echo**.

- When the chopping board is covered with a tea towel, the sound is much quieter - because sounds reflect better off hard surfaces than off soft ones.

- If you have ever been in a completely empty house - one which has no carpets, curtains or furniture - you will know that it sounds quite spooky. The sound of your footsteps echoes off all the hard surfaces - making it sound like there is someone else there as well. Once the house is full of soft things - like carpets and furniture - you don't usually hear any echoes.

Now try this

- Find a large, empty plastic or metal bin. (Make sure it isn't a smelly one!) Put your head just a little way inside and say 'HELLO'. Did you hear an echo?

- If you can't find a clean bin, a large cardboard box usually works quite well.

- Put some towels around the sides and bottom of the bin and try again. Do you still get an echo?

Fun Facts: Seeing with Sound - Ultrasound

- **Ultrasound** is a word used to describe very high frequency sounds. These sounds are far too high-pitched for humans to hear.

- Doctors use ultrasound to examine a foetus inside a mother's womb.

- The doctor holds a small device which produces ultrasound against the mother's stomach. The ultrasound reflects off the foetus.

- The device detects the reflected sounds - and a computer is used to convert the reflected sounds into a picture.

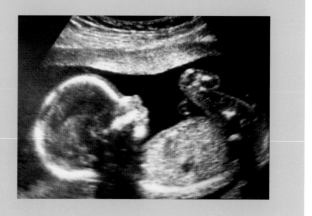

Fun Facts: Seeing with Sound - Echolocation

- Since bats usually fly at night they use something called **echolocation** to help them to 'see' where they are going in the dark.

- They send out very high-pitched sounds - which bounce back off anything which is in their way.

- By listening out for the reflected sounds they can avoid flying into trees and houses.

- They can even hear the tiny echo produced when the sound bounces off an insect. So bats also use sound to help them catch insects - which they eat.

What have we found out?

- An echo occurs when a sound is reflected off a surface.

- Sounds are usually reflected better from hard surfaces than from soft surfaces.

53

Bag-Pipes

In this experiment we are going to make some bagpipes. Okay, I admit that they don't really sound like the traditional Scottish instrument - but they are made with just a bag and a pipe.

How to make your Bag-Pipes

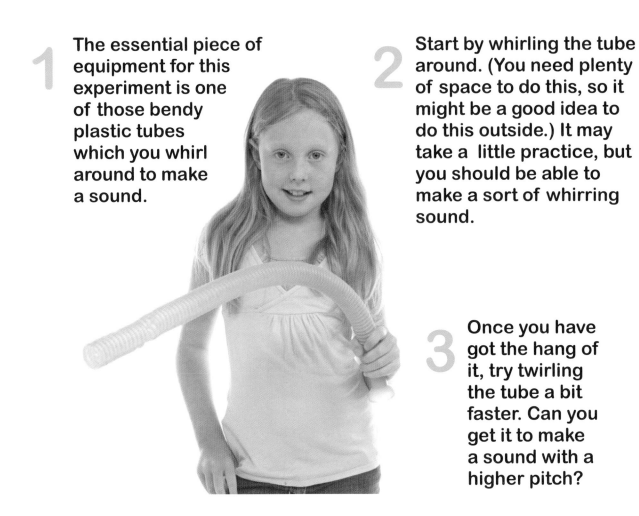

1 The essential piece of equipment for this experiment is one of those bendy plastic tubes which you whirl around to make a sound.

2 Start by whirling the tube around. (You need plenty of space to do this, so it might be a good idea to do this outside.) It may take a little practice, but you should be able to make a sort of whirring sound.

3 Once you have got the hang of it, try twirling the tube a bit faster. Can you get it to make a sound with a higher pitch?

4 You can also try twirling it really slowly. If you get the speed just right it will make a sound with a really low pitch.

5 Now we are going to make the bag-pipes. The first thing to do is to fill the bag with air. (One way to do this is to hold the bag at the top and swish your other hand around inside the bag.)

6 Put one end of your whirling tube into the bag leaving about half of the tube sticking out of the top. Scrunch the top of the bag around the tube. Be careful not to squeeze any air out of the bag as you do this.

7 Hold the bag tightly around the pipe - you don't want any air to escape this way - and ask a friend to squeeze the bag gently. You should hear some strange whistling sounds as the air is forced up the pipe.

8 If it doesn't work, fill the bag with air and try again. You may need to try a couple of times before you get it to work. Try squeezing the bag harder or more gently and you will discover that the sounds change.

55

Now try this

In this experiment we are going to make a Bull-Roarer. All you need is a 30cm ruler and a length of string about 1m long.

- Ask an adult to drill a small hole near one end of the ruler. (You may find that there is already a hole near the end - in which case just use that.)

- Thread one end of the string through the hole and tie it securely. (It might be a good idea to ask an adult to do this as you need to make sure that the knot won't come undone.)

- At the other end of the string make a small loop.

- Put your hand through the loop in the string and swing the ruler round above your head as fast as you can. Make sure you don't hit yourself - or anyone else - with it. (It might be a good idea to do this outside where there is plenty of space.)

- When you swing it round your bull-roarer should make a low-pitched whirring sound. (If you can't hear it, you need to spin the bull-roarer faster.)

Fun Facts: Aboriginal Bull-Roarers

- Bull-roarers have been used for thousands of years. One has been found which is nearly 20 000 years old.

- They are made by many people all over the world - including Australian Aborigines.

- The low-pitched sounds made by a bull-roarer can travel several kilometres - so they were often use by people to communicate with each other.

- Paul Hogan uses a bull-roarer in the film Crocodile Dundee II.

How does it work?

We have made sounds in several different ways in these experiments, so we will look at how each one works.

Whirling Tubes

- When you spin a whirling tube, air travels through the tube. If you cover the end of the tube - or squeeze hard on the end so that no air can get through - the sound stops. So the sound is caused by air moving though the tube.

- As the air hits the ridges in the tube, it bounces off in different directions. This makes the air **vibrate**.

- If you spin the tube faster, the air travels through the tube more quickly, making a sound with a **higher pitch**.

- You may have noticed that the pitch does not change continuously as you whirl the tube faster. Instead it jumps from one pitch to another. This is because the air in the tube can only vibrate at certain **frequencies**.

Bag-Pipes

- When we squeeze the bag, air gets forced through the tube. So we can make the air go through the tube without having to whirl it around.

- If you squeeze harder, the air is pushed through faster. This has the same effect as spinning the tube faster - it makes the pitch higher.

Bull-Roarer

- When you twirl the bull-roarer above your head, the piece of wood spins around on its axis. (You may be able to see it spinning as it slows down.)

- As the wood spins around it pushes the air apart and then squeezes it together. If you do it at just the right speed, the air vibrates - which makes a sound.

What have we found out?

- **We can make sounds by making air vibrate.**

Glossary

This section explains the meanings of some words associated with Sound. Most of these words are used in this book.

Amplify - When we **amplify** a sound it means making the sound **louder**. For example, in the *Laughing Chicken* experiment we found that the yogurt pot amplifies the sound.

Diaphragm - (pronounced 'di-a-fram') A **diaphragm** is a thin, stretched surface which can be made to **vibrate**. In the *Dancing Krispies* experiment the diaphragm was made from a freezer bag. The rubber balloon in the *Balloon Bassoon* experiment also acts as a diaphragm.

Ear Drum - The **ear drum** is a thin film of skin inside your ear which **vibrates** when a sound enters your ear. If you damage your eardrum, it will not vibrate properly - and your hearing will be impaired. The proper medical name for the eardrum is tympanic membrane.

Echo - An **echo** occurs when a sound **reflects** off something and bounces back to you. We investigated echoes in the *Bouncing Sounds* experiment.

Echolocation - (pronounced 'eko-low-kay-shun') - This means using **reflected** sounds (or **echoes**) to find your way around. Bats use **echolocation** so that they can fly in the dark without bumping in to things. Some other animals, such as dolphins and whales, also use echolocation.

Frequency - The **frequency** measures how fast something **vibrates**. It means more or less the same thing as the word **pitch**. Frequency is measured in a unit called Hertz (Hz). A frequency of 100Hz means that the object is vibrating backwards and forwards one hundred times every second.

High - When a sound has a **high pitch** it means that something is **vibrating** quickly. High-pitched sounds are usually quite squeaky. We have found out in many of these experiments that sounds with a high pitch are usually caused by something small vibrating.

Loud - This means that the sound is very noisy. **Loud** means the opposite of **quiet**.(Make sure you don't confuse **loud** with **low**.)

Loudspeaker - A **loudspeaker** is something which converts an electrical signal into a sound that we can hear. You usually find loudspeakers on televisions, CD players and radios. Earphones are also loudspeakers - they are just really tiny ones. Large loudspeakers can produce much louder sounds than small ones.

Low - When a sound has a **low pitch** it means that something is **vibrating** slowly. Low-pitched sounds are usually made when something large vibrates. (Make sure you don't confuse **low-pitched** sounds with **loud** sounds.)

Microphone - A **microphone** is used to convert sounds into electrical signals. We need to use a microphone if we want to record our voice onto a CD or a computer. We speak into a microphone every time we use a telephone or a mobile phone.

Molecule - Gases, liquids and most solids are made up of tiny particles called **molecules**. A molecule is so tiny that it cannot be seen even with a powerful microscope.

Muffle - When we **muffle** a sound we make it **quieter**. In the *Be Quiet!* experiment we used bubble wrap (and some other materials) to muffle the sound.

Percussion - **Percussion** instruments are musical instruments which you hit - like a drum or a cymbal. The *Crisp Tube Bonkos* are also percussion instruments.

Pitch - The **pitch** of a sound means whether the sound is **high** or **low**. Scientists often use the word **frequency** rather than **pitch**.

Quiet - A **quiet** sound is one that you can only just hear. **Quiet** is the opposite of **loud**. In the *Super Hearing* experiment we used a tube to help us hear a really quiet sound.

Reflect - When a sound is **reflected** from a surface it usually produces an **echo**. We investigated the reflection of sounds in the *Bouncing Sounds* experiment. (We also use this word to describe what happens when light bounces off a shiny surface, such as a mirror.)

Sound Source - A **sound source** is something that makes a sound. Musical instruments and loudspeakers are sound sources. Many of the things that we have made in this book - including the *Laughing Chicken*, the *Balloon Bassoon* and the *Straw Oboe* - are also sound sources.

Sound Waves - Scientists often talk about **sound waves** when they describe how a sound travels. Sound waves are not really like the type of wave that crashes onto a beach. They are more like the ripples on a pond.

Stethoscope - A **stethoscope** is an instrument that a doctor uses to listen to sounds inside your body. We made a stethoscope using a hosepipe in the *Super Hearing* experiment.

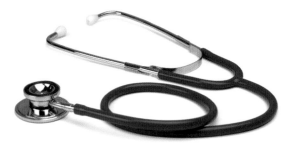

Stringed Instrument - Violins, double basses and guitars (including our *Elastic Band Guitar*) are all examples of **stringed instruments**. These instruments are played either by plucking the strings or by playing them with a bow. The 'strings' are not really made from string - they are usually made of plastic or wire.

Tension - We can change the **pitch** of a sound by altering the **tension** of a string or drum skin. If you increase the tension, the pitch gets higher. Decrease the tension and the pitch becomes lower.

Timbre - The same musical note played on two different instruments has a different sound quality or **timbre**.

Tuning - If we **tune** a musical instrument we change the **pitch** of the sound so that it plays musical notes. When an orchestra is **tuning up**, each musician is trying to make sure that his or her instrument plays a sound with the same pitch as all the others.

Ultrasound - **Ultrasound** means sound which has such a **high frequency** (or high **pitch**) that it is too high for humans to hear. Ultrasound has a frequency of more than 20 000 Hz. This means that whatever is making the sound needs to **vibrate** back and forth more than 20 000 times every second.

Vibration - When something is moving backwards and forwards we say that it is **vibrating**. If anything is making a sound, it must be vibrating - although usually the vibrations are too small for us to see.

Volume - The **volume** of a sound means whether it is **loud** or **quiet**.

Notes for Parents and Teachers

Hi Mums, Dads and teachers, these pages are especially for you.

Whilst the experiments in this book have been designed to be fun for children (and hopefully for adults too), each experiment also helps to reinforce a particular scientific principle.

The book is aimed primarily at supporting the education of children in Primary Science (i.e. aged 5 to 11), although some of the experiments are suitable for younger children whilst others could also provide benefit for older ones. In particular, these two pages illustrate how the experiments could be used to support the **National Curriculum for England, Wales and Northern Ireland** and the Scottish **Environmental Studies: 5-14 National Guidelines**, but the topics are relevant to most other national frameworks of primary science.

Relevance to the National Curriculum for England, Wales and Northern Ireland

Science QCA Unit 1F - Sound and Hearing (typically age 5-6 years)
The most suitable experiments for this unit are:

Crisp Tube Bonkos	Laughing Chicken	Elastic Band Guitar
Straw Oboe	Super Hearing	Where's That Sound?
Ringing In Your Ears	Be Quiet!	Dancing Krispies

Listening to sounds / Making different sounds / Describing sounds
- Crisp Tube Bonkos, Laughing Chicken, Elastic Band Guitar, Straw Oboe
These experiments provide several different ways of making sounds (e.g. by hitting, blowing, rubbing, plucking) and allow many different words to be used to describe and compare the sounds (e.g. quiet, loud, low, high, quieter, higher, etc).
How we hear - recognising that we hear sounds through our ears, and that our ears give us information about where sounds are coming from - Where's That Sound?, Ringing In Your Ears, Be Quiet!
Sound and distance - Super Hearing.
(Although the link between vibration and sound is not a specific part of this unit, some children will be able to make this connection - and they will all enjoy watching the Dancing Krispies.)

Science QCA Unit 5F - Changing Sounds (typically age 9-10 years)
The most suitable experiments for this unit are:

Laughing Chicken	*Elastic Band Guitar*	*Straw Oboe*
Super Hearing	*Ringing In Your Ears*	*Be Quiet!*
Dancing Krispies	*Balloon Bassoon*	*Make An Ear*
Bouncing Sounds	*Bag-Pipes*	

Observing how sound is made - sounds are made when objects vibrate
- *Laughing Chicken, Elastic Band Guitar, Straw Oboe, Ringing In Your Ears, Dancing Krispies, Make An Ear, Balloon Bassoon, Bag-Pipes*
Vibrations and sound / How sound travels - vibrations from sound sources travel through different materials to reach the ear - *Laughing Chicken, Super Hearing, Ringing In Your Ears, Bouncing Sounds*
Preventing sound travelling / How to muffle sound - *Be Quiet!*
Describing sounds / Changing sounds - investigating change in pitch
- *Laughing Chicken, Elastic Band Guitar, Straw Oboe, Balloon Bassoon, Bag-Pipes*
Pitch in stringed instruments - *Elastic Band Guitar*
Pitch in wind instruments - *Straw Oboe*
(Although this unit does not specifically deal with echoes or the concept of reflecting sounds, pupils at this age are all familiar with the phenomenon of echoes - in fact, many of them misuse the term - and they are also familiar with the concept of reflection of light.)

Several of these experiments are also relevant to **Design and Technology Unit 5A: Musical Instruments**

Relevance to Scotland - Environmental Studies: 5-14 National Guidelines - Society, Science and Technology

Energy and Forces - Properties and uses of Energy
Level A - Sources of sound - *Crisp Tube Bonkos, Laughing Chicken, Elastic Band Guitar, Straw Oboe*
Level B - Link between sound and hearing - *Ringing In Your Ears, Where's That Sound?, Be Quiet!*
Level C - Link between sound and vibration - *Laughing Chicken, Elastic Band Guitar, Ringing In Your Ears, Dancing Krispies, Balloon Bassoon, Make An Ear, Bag-Pipes*
Level D - Use of 'pitch' and 'volume' - *Laughing Chicken, Elastic Band Guitar, Straw Oboe, Balloon Bassoon, Bag-Pipes*
Level E - Sound passing through various materials - *Laughing Chicken, Super Hearing, Ringing In Your Ears, Be Quiet!*
Level F - Relationship between pitch and frequency and between loudness and amplitude - *Dancing Krispies* (by turning up the volume of the CD player you can make the krispies jump higher.)

About Professor Brainstorm

'Is your real name Professor Brainstorm?' It's a question which I get asked often by chidren - and sometimes by adults. Well, I'm sorry to disappoint you. Unfortunately, my parents were not called Mr and Mrs Brainstorm. But although I am not really Professor Brainstorm, I am a real scientist.

My interest in science probably started around the time that Neil Armstrong and Edwin Aldrin landed on the Moon. I was at junior school at the time, and I was fascinated by space. When I left school, I was still interested in science. I went to Newcastle University to study Physics, and a few years later I took a PhD in Physics as well. About this time I also discovered that I enjoyed teaching other people about how the world works, so for several years I taught science to university students.

In 2002 I decided that I wanted to do more to get younger children interested in science. So I started doing science shows in schools - and changed my name to Professor Brainstorm.

This book shows you how to do some of the experiments from my shows - and lots of other fun experiments too. The great thing about science is that you don't need to go to the Moon or do something incredibly complicated to learn about how the world works. The experiments in this book use very simple pieces of equipment - and yet they can teach you some incredible things. Although I have been a scientist for many years, some of these experiments amazed me the first time I tried them. Some of them continue to amaze me - even though I have done them hundreds of times before.

So I hope you have as much fun doing these experiments as I have had putting them all together.

Additional picture credits (all iStockphoto Picture Library):
4a Grafissimo 2006; 4b Peter Finnie 2007; 5a Nancy Honeycutt 2007; 16a franckreporter 2009; 16b Sergii Sukhorukov 2009; 17b Phil Berry 2004; 17c Diane White Rosier 2006; 20a Terry Wilson 2007; 32 Marcin Pawinski 2008; 33b Feng Yu 2009; 36a Eliza Snow 2007; 41a Soubrette 2007; 49a/60b Don Bayley 2008; 49d Jim Jurica 2006; 49c Steve Cole 2007; 53 Isabelle Limbach 2007; 58b Carmen Martinez Banus 2008; 58c Pavlo Maydikov 2007; 59a Nina Shannon 2006; 59b Stas Perov 2007; 59c Krzysztof Kwiatkowski 2007; 60a Philip Dyer 2009; 60d David Joyner 2008; 61a James Steidl 2006; 61b Ian Hubball 2009; 61c Alex Potemkin 2008

Last but not least, a big thank you to the models - Sophie, Joseph and Oscar.